Great Man Theory

Trevor Blake

mogtus-sanlux

2024

Great Man Theory by Trevor Blake

© 2024 Trevor Blake. All rights reserved.

Cover: *Halo with Three Parhelia, Winter Harbour Melville Island* by Charles Hamilton Smith.

mogtus-sanlux 325

~mogtus-sanlux

mogtus-sanlux.one

Blake, Trevor

[English]

Great Man Theory

ISBN 978-1-944651-34-3

1. Philosophy

2. History

Trevor Blake (b. 1966)

127 House: At every turn in its thought society will find us — waiting.

Great Man Theory

History is the echo

of individual men

who have shouted.

I.

I have a certain advantage in writing *Great Man Theory*. Not being a Great Man myself, I may observe the field in full at a distance.

I have the advantage that my book will be fine, if not first, as there are few books on the topic. For this reason I may overstate my case in comfort, as the few other books on the topic rush to mention exceptions to the rule. Most books on Great Man Theory contain as much matter in favor of other theories as they do for Great Man Theory.

These other authors may present Great Man Theory, but then call to the stage theories of Gods, theories of masses, theories of classes, and insist that we clap for them as well. Most books are either neutral or antagonistic to Great Man Theory. Therefore I grant myself license to write of Great Man Theory with bravado, leaving the alternatives to others.

I have one more advantage in writing *Great Man Theory*. I have clarity that Great Man Theory describes this world and the men in it as they are, and it is not a prescription on how this world and the world "might" be or "should" be. Great Man theory is indifferent if anyone believes it, in the way that it is indifferent to sound if you prefer silence.

Let me clean house before I invite in this great company with a few words on what Great Man Theory is not.

I offer no checklist for identifying a Great Man, nor becoming one. I admit every contradiction and omission as able to identify itself. Reading a recipe suits my taste, but I write of feasts. This book is more like a song than a chemical formula, calling for a dance and not curing a disease.

Lying and murder can unstitch a Great Man, but there is no Frankenstein process to stitch one together. The Great Man will not be pinned to a board in a collection, even if he is nailed to a cross. The contradictions and the repetitions are noted and deliberate and left as I found them.

Great Man Theory is not a theory of laws. Great Men produce laws, but laws do not produce Great Men. There is no legislating a Great Man into existence, no authorizing body to license Great Men. Great Men collide as often as they collaborate. They measure and are not measured.

Praise alone does not make for Great Men. The generations of men who venerated their Kings for being Kings did not make them Great Men, and the generations of men who despise Kings for being Kings do not reduce (some few of) them from being Great Men. It is not a medal, but mettle, which can make a Great Man.

Great Man Theory is not a theory of the gods. History as the drama of the gods is an older theory, a recommendation to consider the theory well. The Gods are said to know us, and often to wish us well, to make us fit to sit at their table. The gods put opportunities and challenges before us, the gods shout out their directions to the world stage. Sometimes the gods will re-cast us in new roles, so confident they are we will succeed.

I know two reasons why Great Man Theory is not a theory of the gods. If the gods do not exist, no further reason is required. If the gods do exist, this very book may be a few lines of their script. My having no means to prove I am other than another of their poor actors, cast in a villain's role, to lie, to deceive, I can only say with certainty the gods are not the subject of this book.

Great Man Theory is not a theory of progress. Progress cannot abide Great Man Theory. Progress cannot allow for any exceptions to itself, for if it cannot progress in every direction then it is no longer progress in one direction. It has a weakness that cannot be hidden, where it has no strength, and that is that progress needs us all to keep falling forward. No man may stand alone, nor stand at all. Standing men are seen as impediments to progress.

Progress demands things are not only changing, but changing for the better, by following a formula. The new formula, so much improved over the old, allows all things to change. Through most of history, Heaven has been either all around us or a kingdom beyond life. Since the *Anno Domini*, Heaven been re-zoned by formula as a place to be made on Earth. It is said if all men join in faith, if all Kings live under the law and not a living man, if all men (and women!) can vote, if we can all just awaken our class consciousness, and most of all if just one more mountain of corpses can be amassed, just this, then justice.

We fall forward in progress only with a gentle if bloody course-correction now and again. We progress, all of us together as one. And if one man should emerge as the new First Citizen each and every time the collective changes, well, it only shows how much further there is to fall.

Some Great Men have shouted "progress!" and it may be difficult to see where they err. Honest and cynical Great Men alike have shouted progress. The difficulty in seeing their error is not due to our sight being blocked by a mountain of corpses, not if we agree that they had it coming to them.

The difficulty for the rest of us in knowing Great Man Theory comes in tuning out the echoes from some of them having shouted about progress. When so many are happy to shout along, or afraid to stop shouting, it is difficult to see that the chorus has a conductor. But listen again, there he is, each time.

And that is enough house-cleaning of what Great Man Theory is not. Elegant and refined or rough and ready, let us now usher in those other books which also speak of our heroes and villains.

A book writes as loudly as the voice of its reader. Some books are silent to me, no matter how they resonate to other men. Leaving aside my advantages in writing a book on Great Man Theory, there are other men who have written before me that I would like to place before you.

The Hero Lectures of Thomas Carlyle, published as *Heroes and Hero Worship* in 1841, are exemplary. I found his book difficult to read, but easy to read aloud. Perhaps you will as well. The Hero Lectures are a survey of Great Men from antiquity to the men of his time, from legend to hard science. The Great Men of the Hero Lectures are Odin (legend), Muhammad (prophet), Dante and Shakespeare (poets), Luther and Knox (priests), Johnson, Rousseau and Burns (authors), and Cromwell and Napoleon (Kings).

These Great Men in Carlyle's book are neatly grouped by themes as well as arranged chronologically. I could do no better than Carlyle and so I say little of any of these Great Men, but I do also group my Great Men by themes and, very roughly, chronologically. Carlyle sings out a song I can only rephrase, never compose. *Hero Worship* introduces his topic, then hails representative men across legend, religion, the arts and the battlefield. Where you see the same in my book, it is no accident. My advice is to read Carlyle's book aloud, as he read it aloud. The rhythms of speech permit what the printed page prohibits.

The Ego and His Own (1845) by Max Stirner is the completion of Western philosophy, as *The Prince* (1532) by Machiavelli is the completion of Western politics. Machiavelli sought favor with royalty by writing a manual for their expedient success. But to give the game away so plainly had the opposite effect, and Machiavelli was the first to be accused of being Machiavellian.

Stirner's goals appear more sound: to amuse himself and to needle his former friends, Karl Marx and Friedrich Engels. In these goals, he succeeded. *The Ego and His Own* carries the conclusion of Protagoras to its happy end. Man is the measure of all things. Not all men, not a man, not even you, but this man, right here, the author of *The Ego and His Own*. Stirner writes all things belong to him, based on his ability to keep others from taking them and his interest in keeping them. And by all "things" Stirner means property, people, time, language, truth, causality... the inclusive sort of "all things."

Was Stirner serious, or did he overstate his case to prove a point? Niezsche may have read Stirner, and other rogue philosophers definitely did. You can read him for yourself and decide for yourself. You well know only you can decide for yourself, and what Stirner writes starts to look more like a mirror. The authors of "The Communist Manifesto" contributed to the enslavement and / or liberation of over half the planet while Stirner died alone, penniless, without a friend and dropped in a pauper's grave.

Those who write about Great Men tend to come to poor ends, while men who act as Great Men have their way. Read Stirner's book as if you wrote it. What he says is true may not convince you, but what he says is false is difficult to forget or argue away.

"Representative Men" is an essay by Ralph Waldo Emerson. He writes in 1850 the word "representative" where a more recent writer might write the opposite word: exemplary. Or, remembering the word means neither good nor bad but *more*, the word Great. "Representative Men" has a brevity already lost to this book. I recommend the book best by saying no more about it.

There is some evidence that Friedrich Nietzsche read Stirner, and some evidence that he did not. In my mind, what Nietzsche wrote stands tall either way. "Thus Spoke Zarathustra" (1883) is the narrative song of a Great Man told in a book. The song of Zarathustra is not for all to hear, and only for one man to sing. It is a song of the radiant and the strong as beset by the dark and misshapen, these not as symbols of good and evil but as good and evil themselves.

Everyone thinks they are the good guy. The mind is more made for rationalizations than rationality. Some men make stories that justify their bad acts as good. And some men say no, they are bad men and their actions are bad, but they are not concerned with rights, only abilities.

Among those men who so helped themselves were the "illegalists" of Italy and France in the late 1800s. They robbed and killed because they wanted to, because they wanted things without paying. They differentiated themselves from other bandits by taunting the police in letters, bragging of their crimes. What was good for them, this was their good.

The secret vigilante is as good and as bad as he judges himself to be, and as good and as bad as others judge him to be. Some are openly murderous, some are quietly altruistic, some a bit of both. I have my views on the Boston Tea Party, the Capirote, the Danites, the Masons, the Assassins, and other secret vigilante groups. These men declared themselves above the law to preserve the law — their law, which they would other men fall under.

I do not call any of these secret vigilantes Great Men. But. Their mode informed the most readily identifiable Great Men of twentieth-century literature, the superhero and the super-villain. The Scarlet Pimpernel, Zorro, Superman, Batman and all that come after, these are Great Men in their great and terrible deeds.

The novels and philosophy of Ayn Rand sing loud hozanas to Great Men and to the heroic in art. Rand held that there were some traits found in all Great Men, and some traits never found in Great Men, and this book can generally agree. Rand also held that the means to be a Great Man, such as a dedication to reason and a respect for property were available to all men, which this book might suggest is not in harmony with the evidence (see "illegalism") and, less important, is not in the canon of Great Man Theory. Everyone can be better but not everyone can be the best, wouldn't you say? Still: read "Atlas Shrugged" (1957).

I have come to accept that I am not only stubborn, but largely ignorant. I hope the reader will accept this as well. I am entirely sure that I am ignorant of many other Great Men who are not in the above works nor in mine. Their exclusion from this book comes only from my ignorance and no for other reason.

I have one last advantage in writing this book. I am a stubborn fool. Men who favor causes, classes, mobs, these are the fashionable men. These are the men who have had their way for centuries. If I were clever I might write a book like *all the other books*. I might join the chorus of the cause. Better still, write no book and *act*. For no book may shout.

Being a stubborn fool, I write. I write of a theory so ignored and hated that no book like it has been written. The mob will have its way, and one thing will come to us all. But like a donkey will bray, I write. This may be my great advantage. Like a donkey far more humble than his burden, I bring you Great Man Theory.

    I have hummed the tune of Great Man Theory so that you may recognize it when you hear it. Look for Great Men, be worthy of them for your own sake. Turn away from the grey pool of the mob, with only slick oils on its surface to give it any distinction. Look up the mountain.

Envoi

A dishonest summary of my book, for dishonest readers.

Those who will review my book without reading it, or having read it will review words I never wrote, will find I have here done their work for them. If you are an honest reader you will find opportunities to criticize my book, and I will thank you for it. And if you are an honest reader and you see the following sentiments in a review of this book, feel free to accuse such critics of plagiarism of this *envoi*, this dishonest summary.

I, the author of *Great Man Theory*, am a Great Man, the Greatest of all Great Men.

Any man not included in this book is not a Great Man. In my infinite wisdom, I have surveyed every fact and fiction and distilled them into this slim volume.

The man who speaks of the world as it is, speaks of the world as he prefers it.

Great Men are all good men, especially that one man. I am definitely saying that every Great Man is a saint, an angel walking among us, and any deed he did or demanded is worthy of praise and honor. The actions of Great Man are good because a Great Man did them. Great has no secondary meaning, such as "large" or "loud," because great in this book only means "good."

All actions are carried out by Great Men. No group, and no woman, has ever acted in any way at any time, and when they did it was foul and failed.

II.

I have imagined what might happen if Great Man Theory overcame the theological and communistic theories of history. The clear answer is that I don't know, and just as clearly the answer is it does not matter. Great Man Theory is not a prescription of how things might be, but a description of things as they are. Great Man Theory is frowned upon only in the past few hundred years. Many still smile upon it, if in secret. It does not matter if Great Man Theory overcomes the theological or communistic theories of history.

It does not matter if Great Man Theory regains the "but of course!" status it held for so much of mankind's history. It does not matter if I believe in Great Man Theory, nor you. It does not matter if only one stubborn fool writes this book, and no one reads it. Great Man Theory is, self-consistently, not dependent on crowds for validation. Although it is largely discredited or forgotten or suppressed, Great Man Theory *exists*. It has powers of explanation and prediction that other theories lack.

The problem with your understanding of the weakness and ugliness and lies of the modern world is that it probably not bad enough. But... what of it? There is no need to read another account of how bad things are, or have been. Remember, Great Men are absolutely not all good men.

If Great Man Theory were the theory of the majority, and Great Men strode the earth in the open, we would have less lies and I would prefer that. We would have more of what I do not prefer as well. Great Man Theory is not here to save you nor to save the world. It's just the world, a world that doesn't need saving after all.

There is a lie told by the weak that makes the world ugly, and that is the lie of equality. It is not that equality does not exist. There is a thing that comes to all men, and that is death. Death is the great equality. It comes to all, and the outcome is the same for all. Death is not terrible, or we would think it so for each of the plants and animals who die so that we might live a little longer. It's also nice to see the death of a person you hate, isn't it.

The lie of equality is not that it does not exist. It is that equality other than death does exist. It is a lie that equality, any sort of sameness or interchangeability, exists. All is change, and nothing remains the same. Even in death there is change as our component parts dissipate.

The existence (or no) of a human essence, a soul, a mind, a "real" you, which does not change from before birth and through life and after death, is your own affair. I do not think I have one of those, and I do not think I am one of those. I am a poor body, minimally maintained and destined for the grave. Equality as sameness does not exist.

Equality as interchangeability also does not exist. Early education in mathematics makes it seem that way, but think again. In mathematics, if you have one and one together, that makes two, and two is interchangeable with one and one. But this math is a description of a thing, not the thing itself. If you have two nice apples, you have one apple and one apple and they are both apples. But they are not interchangeable, they are not indistinguishable from each other, and there is no "two-ness" about them.

There is a "two" there in the same way there is a "nice" about them; it is something we say about the apples, but it is not the apples. An apple and an orange are two fruit, not interchangeable in other ways. An apple and an egg may be two objects on a table, and they not interchangeable in other ways. I have imagined what might happen if we could perceive and speak of those two nice apples directly, without language. Now that would be something indeed.

I have a preference for my own kind, and I will leave the produce behind on the table. My kind is mankind. Some say that men are equal in their sameness and interchangeability. But they say a confused lie. Some say well yes, men are not all the same, nor are they interchangeable, but as a whole men are equal. Some men are good at this task, some are good at another task, and as a whole men average out to equality. The evidence that as a whole men are equal is available to anyone who will only study one man, and only for a short period of study. Some men are good at nearly everything they set out to do. There are not many of them.

Some men are not able to achieve any of their goals, and they may not have the self-reflection capacities to have goals. I am thinking of men who are profoundly mentally ill, or who have organic brain damage. Before you rush to say these men don't count, consider whose company you will keep by doing so. These men are neither good nor bad for their abilities, they are just themselves as each man is himself. Most men do have areas of proficiency. But not all areas of proficiency are the same or interchangeable, not to honest men.

The difference between being skilled at writing a book about Great Man Theory and the skills of being a Great Man are profound. The former has nearly no influence in the world, while the later is the prime mover of the world.

The communists say that history is a record of class struggle. Nomadic hunters and gatherers clashed against early farmers. The excess resources of the farmers won out. The farmers winning out led to feudalism. The feudalists clashed against the early capitalists. The accuracy of capitalist data won out. The capitalists winning out led to capitalism. Capitalism has accurate records of how many apples, oranges and eggs a society needs, but the inequalities of capitalism are leading to a clash with the communists.

And the communists will break the chain of class conflict (say the communists). The communists will win because communism, and they will not struggle against themselves. By using of the records kept by the capitalists on what a society needs, but distributing it according to need instead of the ability to pay, a final state of history will be achieved.

All of history is class struggle, except when it isn't. Clashes between classes inevitably lead to communism, except when it doesn't (and let's agree at least that it has not yet). The communist bait and switch is as plain or as complex as you wish it to be. But even if the class struggle theory of history were true, and even if all men were communists, their proposal is doomed.

A record of many apples, oranges and eggs a society needs is accurate until the inevitable changes of life. A blight that wipes out a season's worth of apples does not make the apples appear just because they are needed. The number of eggs needed by a society might be entirely stable, if eugenic measures are taken to keep the population steady and if travel were restricted to a well-enforced egg zone.

We have some records that show on average how little air is necessary for a man to stay alive. But how many apples does a man need? What of men who just don't like apples, or have an allergy, or a religious objection to them? Will the State let their quota of apples rot, or redistribute them according to... what standard? The word "need" smuggles in the idea *prefer*, nearly every time.

Even if families could be forced or dispatched on central command, even if borders were as rigid as the walls of a prison cell, and even if men accepted the sacrifices of communism as less than the benefits, a final poison enters the formula. The accurate records of the needs of society end when communism begins. Any resource devoted to free inquiry is a resource not known to produce results and therefore a waste. No new inventions can happen after communism, nor exploration.

The Communist Manifesto was published in 1848. If the accurate records of capitalism had been frozen at that time, we would have no refrigeration, no heavier than air controlled flight, no computers, no internet, we would have nothing that capitalism had not already provided accurate records for by 1848. If waste is allowed with fingers crossed that something good will come, then the accurate records of the capitalists were not so accurate after all.

If waste is allowed but measured by new record keeping, the communists will have to devise some objective measure as to how much or little the waste produced. Perhaps they could use small discs of metal, or specially printed rectangles of paper, or digital ledger sheets. And so communism resolves itself to the market, just as it has in every attempt at communism.

Poverty exists, lots of it, and it always has. A little wealth exists, more of it than has ever existed. There's no reason we couldn't all go back to being nomadic hunters and gatherers again, if "we all" is understood to be a few billion less of us in the world of the living. The communists define the working class as those who labor but who do not own the means of production of their own labor. Spare a moment to think of the athletes and actors and software writers who are billionaires many times over, none of whom own the means of production of their own labor. According to the communists these unfortunates are just as oppressed as a child slave digging blood diamonds from the mud.

Classes are so easy to define backwards in time that all definitions work well. Consider how the communists defined their class as the best, and grant yourself the same franchise. Poverty and wealth, social compassion and social exploitation, individual needs and social needs, all of these exist in plain fact without the gloss of class.

Newborn infants turn to their mother's voice more than other voices, and they turn to those speaking their mother's language more than to other languages. Newborn infants turn to human faces more than any other visual stimulus, and turn to symmetrical images more than a-symmetrical images. None of this is taught, or cultural. It is inborn, and pre-born. Those preferences are strong evidence that what is thought of as worthy of attention, as preferred, as beautiful, is not entirely taught and not entirely cultural.

It is a happy coincidence, perhaps, that all of the universe seems to prefer symmetry. There are universal gestural expressions. Shyness / attraction conveyed by looking down and then to the side. Aggression conveyed by making oneself appear larger. All humans wear some kind of clothing and adornment, groom hair, cook food. In the larger perspective, there are no exceptions.

When you get down to the individual level, we are all a bunch of weirdos. Is it a meaningful statement to say we're all equally unequal? Or that we're all alike in being different? That a thing is equal to itself at the time of observation and in the means measured is so true it is a fine axiom, but just you wait one moment more and we're back to a thing not even being equal to itself (are you the baby you were or the cadaver you will be?).

Clothing is not (just) a temperature valve. People in the warmest regions have no need for it, but wear it anyway. There were people in Northern Europe, one of the coldest regions, who wore little clothing, instead keeping warm by smearing themselves with bear grease. It's possible to eat a raw diet for a full lifetime but it is an individualized exception when that happens. The rest of us cook our food. Inborn traits are in evidence for humans.

I think we are natural beings, not supernatural beings. I do not think there is a soul, or a mind, or a "real" me that isn't just me. So... do we have free will? Maybe this is a malformed question. Maybe it does not matter. I tend to think that human ignorance is sufficient to stand in for free will.

We could know the consequence of all choices, but we do not, and that is a pretend sort of free will. It seems both reasonable and lovely to think there is objective beauty. And objective ugliness? Well, subvocalization happens all the time. We hear sound, and our vocal apparatus mimics it. Sudden loud sounds and some other sounds cause a very physical choking sensation. This is objective ugliness in sound. Those who survive full-body third degree burns are objectively ugly, just ask them.

There is objective ugliness, and only ugly souls will say there is no objective beauty. I might laugh at the idea of divine rights, royal rights, natural rights and human rights, but substitute "right" for "ability" and the argument has weight. I have no right for or against gravity, only an ability (at this time) to rise up when I fall down. I do not say that a Great Man will have a right to do what he does, only that he has the ability to do what he does.

Allow that differences among men exist, have always existed, will always exist, and these differences will include the trivial and the profound. Allow further that given a finite lifetime, which you must know that you do, you do not have infinite time to lift up all men equally, you must act for some men and not for others. You will chose more to your longer preference (or dare I say correctly) if you better yourself as well as other men. Do all you can to not be tricked. Be worthy of yourself, be worthy of better men, and be worthy of a Great Man when you hear his call.

III.

Legends are re-told, never told. The roots of a legend are hidden while the trunk and branches are strong: uproot a legend to see its origins and you kill it. No first-hand account of legends exists, nor should exist. Origins are interesting, excellence is important. Some shouts of history were made so long ago that only the echo of the echo remains. A modern remarkable act is therefore described as legendary, of a kind with a legend, but not a legend. One beat is merely a sound, while many beats make a rhythm. And so legends are re-told.

A legend is not only a matter of fact. There is no evidence in legend, even when there may be fact. No proof, while there may be truth. It takes an especially soured soul to hear a fable of Aesop and say "yes, but animals cannot talk, can they." Demand that there be no tales of talking animals, that there be no legends, and enjoy your own company. There are even Sour Soul Societies for you to join and congratulate each other for joining.

A legend does not live for being true, nor useful. Legends roll through canyon walls on their own wings, radiating their own heat. To look too closely at them is to be blind to what they illuminate. Legends are a reminder that truth is not the good, but a good. Strength is also a good. Beauty is also a good.

Truth, strength and beauty are the natural good, and all who seek to destroy them do evil.

The moral to a story is not virtuous because it is a truth, a truth smuggled in the lie of a story, but because to do the opposite of the moral is ugly and weak.

Hear the Great Men of legend. Some Great Men of legend hold their claim for being true, others for their treachery. Some Great Men of legend are strong, and some are eternally shamed for their weakness. Some Great Men of legend are beautiful, some are known known for their sour souls. Hear the Great Men of legend and what resonates by their passage.

The pagan faiths were of the natural world. They observed gods and spirits we may not see, but these too were natural. The sylphs were of their woods, the gods were of their (far away) halls, prayer was a preference for favor from forces with their own nature. The gods are more than men, in the sense they have greater powers and passions, but their greater passions and powers sometimes have them, and from this comes the fires and floods that consume men. The gods of pre-history were pagan gods. They are in nature, as natural gods.

The natural world is a pagan world. We observe the world and we observe ourselves and we make stories that describe and predict the way of the world and our own ways. When those stories do not match what we observe, the stories can be retained or the stories can be changed. A story that does not change is a tradition. Stories about stories are traditions.

One story about stories is that a story can be changed. The traditional story that stories can be changed is science. Science comes from observations in the pagan world, but is devoted to casting out stories that are false rather than upholding observations that appear true.

The pagan gods of pre-history were natural gods. The gods on this side of history are *super*-natural gods. They exist outside of time and space. Science chased them there, in a hunt that went something like this. There was a man in our tribe who was a God, but he was seen to be man. God was then in the forests, but we went in the forest and saw no God. God ran to the mountaintop, but when we got there, God was gone. God was in the sky for a long time, but we looked and later went to the sky and beyond and there was no God. And so God is no place we can go to, no time we can meet, He is not in nature but superior to nature, the uncreated Creator.

For this there is no counter-argument in evidence, only logic. It was logic that got us to a supernatural God in the first place. I will say again that before the supernatural, the gods were natural, pagan gods. One of them was a Great Man of legend.

The actions of the supernatural Gods are good because they are their actions, not subject to the natural good of truth, strength and beauty. The supernatural gods may delight in us or despise us, but they do not need us, nor need anything. The gods of pre-history, the gods of legend, the pagan gods, are gods of Great Men.

The supernatural gods are closed off from us. I, in turn, will close myself off from them after this chapter. I will write of Hercules as a hero, a representative man, a Great Man of legend.

Hercules was the son of a mortal woman and Zeus, the god of gods. Hera, the primary wife of Zeus, hated his bastard son. She sent two vipers to poison him, but the infant Hercules strangled them in his chubby little hands. Hercules grew in strength and virtue. Hera assaulted Hercules again, this time with a fit of madness in which he killed his beloved family. Seeking penance, Hercules consulted an oracle at a temple to Zeus.

The oracle told him he must serve under a weak king, Eurystheus, for twelve years. King Eurystheus told him he had to complete twelve heroic deeds as his penance. The proof that Eurystheus was a weak king was that when he said the tasks were heroic, Eurystheus meant they were impossible — to him. The weak will praise the weak, the ugly will praise the ugly, and the liar will praise the liar, so that they may keep their faces turned from natures' good.

The weak King Eurystheus thought the natural good of strength was impossible. To abdicate his responsibilities as a King to guide Hercules to penance, Eurystheus set him to what he thought were impossible tasks.

The first great labor was to kill the Lion of Nema. Hercules did so handily, then wore its skin as a cloak. In this, Hercules is the first costumed vigilante, the first Superman.

The second great labor was to slay the Hydra of Lerna. Hercules not only killed the monster, but he burned it so that it could not heal and added its poisonous blood to his arsenal. A Great Man will turn all adversity to his own advantage.

The third great labor was to capture the Boar of Erymanthus. The fourth great labor was to tame the Stag of Arcadia. The fifth great labor was to drive away the Birds of Lake Stymphalus. A Great Man may be called upon (or elect) to kill, but he will be greater still if he has the skill also to domesticate, to civilize.

The sixth great labor was to clean the horse stable of King Augeas. Sometimes to be a Great Man is merely to get rid of a large amount of... refuse.

The seventh great labor was to slay the Bull of Minos. The eighth great labor was to bring the horses of King Diomedes to

King Eurystheus. These horses had been raised to eat human flesh. To control their hunger, Hercules fed them the flesh of King Diomedes. A Great Man can turn his enemy's weapons against him.

The ninth great labor was to seize the Belt of Hippolyta, Queen of the Amazons. He subdued her and took her belt in battle. From this the reader may conclude any suitable lesson on Great Men and goddesses.

The tenth great labor was to seize the cattle guarded by the monster Geryon. The eleventh great labor was to steal the Golden Apples of Hesperides from the Garden of Paradise. The twelfth great labor was to enter Hades, world of the dead, and bring its guardian into the world of the living. By wrestling Cerberus, the three-headed dog, out of the underworld, death then held no power over Hercules. Hercules was a man born of a mortal woman and the King of Kings, who later defeated death itself. A legend not unlike a later legend of another son of another God.

Having completed his twelve labors during his twelve years of service, Hercules completed his penance for his sins. He was freed to choose his own adventure, and joined Jason and the Argonauts as they sought the Golden Fleece.

He married again, this time to Princess Deianira. A centaur tried to rape Deianira, and Hercules killed him with an arrow.

The tip of the arrow had been dipped in the poison blood of the Hydra, gathered in his second great labor. The dying centaur told Deianira that if the affections of Hercules ever strayed, that his own blood, now seeping from his arrow wound, would turn Hercules back toward Deianira. Hercules did stray and did know another Princess.

Deianira applied the centaur's blood to Hercules' cloak, made from the skin of the Lion of Nema, gathered during his first great labor. Hercules put on the cloak. His flesh began to boil and Hercules collapsed in great pain. He had been touched by the blood of the centaur, which had mixed with the poison of the Hydra, which had been added to the tip of the arrow which had been shot by Hercules. The very actions of a Great Man can bring him down. Hercules had himself burned alive to escape the pain. His body was consumed. Having been born of a divine father, having stolen the apples from the tree of life, having wrestled the guardian of the underworld, Hercules died a man and was reborn a god.

The cult of Hercules began in Greece and from there spread to Rome. His legend echoed across the Roman empire and across Europe. One may consider the club of Hercules and the hammer of Thor as two fine strikers. His legend traveled up the Silk Road where his stories and local stories blended.

The natural gods are no more or less distant from us today than they were before. But public temples to Hercules and Zeus are long given to ruin. There is no means to join his cult today. But consider how your life might be different if you could. Some men may take this as a call to form or join a new cult of Hercules. I have no disagreement with them.

Other men may give themselves great labors of strength, truth and beauty, of duty and of penance, and silently carry them out in the service of Hercules. Religion may be a private thing, but it is definitely a secret thing.

And some men will not be moved by the legend of Hercules at all. To these men I say find the legend that does move you. Do not be as a corpse while you live. The legends of every time and place are yours. To believe or not believe or to pretend to believe — these are the wrong dividing lines for legends. If a lack of truth of a legend of a Great Man is holding you back, look for the strength of the legend, or the beauty, and listen, and act.

Men have monsters to slay, including their own worst aspects. Including each other. The Latin phrase *homo homini lupus est* may be translated as "man is a wolf to man." But not all monsters, nor all men, must be slain.

Some monsters may be tamed. Other monsters will be addressed by other men. Deeds of legend cannot be made to order in a one-click cart. While not all legends suit all men, and while deeds of legend chose the man and not the man the deed, the legends of Great Men serve in the telling.

The act of learning the legend that rings for you like a clear bell, and the act of telling it in your own words, is a worthy act. It is good for men to listen and to laugh together. Legends are an agreement to watch each other, hold each other accountable. To be the kind of man who honors the words in his mouth. And not the other kind.

IV.

New social forms do not replace old social forms, but add to them. Agriculture did not entirely erase hunting and gathering, nor did industry do away with agriculture. Theater endures despite radio, radio despite television, television despite cable, cable despite the internet. Legends are those stories that live anew being told anew, and legends too are joined by new forms.

The reason one group is called a religion and another group is called a cult is this: a wish to praise one and deplore the other. In their details and histories, they are of a kind.

The pagan cults were of nature, and did not conceive of a need to determine if their legends were true. The mainstream religions of today, such as Judaism, Christianity and Islam, have a God cast outside of nature, and in an effort to return to that paradise invented mainstream science.

All stories as to cause and effect are alike to a point. The story that a rainbow is light reflecting through water suspended in the sky is equal to the story that a rainbow is God's promise to not destroy the world by flood a second time. These stories are both stories.

The difference between the stories does not come through observation alone. Direct observation will be directed away from potentially relevant events, and indirect observation (what we have been told or heard) are more stories. The difference between stories does not come through observation.

Any test to determine what is true may be the lucky or unlucky one where a false positive is observed, one which confirms the test but which does not confirm the truth. In all of human history, only one means has been invented to differentiate some stories from others. This means is only a few hundred years old, largely unpopular, and may be readily suppressed or ignored.

The means to differentiate some stories from others is the awkwardly named process of falsification. Do not only try to observe a story, nor to test a story to observe if it is true. Imagine a story that explains or describes or predicts, then imagine what what could be observed to make that story false. Not true, but false. This is the means to differentiate some stories from others.

Remove as many extraneous variables as you can. If what you observe does not conform to what would make your story false, you can consider it provisionally true. Provisional truth is good enough to put men on the moon and return them to Earth. Absolute truth is above the capacity of this author.

The story of falsification was first told by Sir Karl Popper. He found predecessors of the story from the time of the cult of Hercules. Falsification can set some stories aside as being provisionally true, but they too may be told again and found to be false or incomplete. The true is not the good, although it can be a good.

Medicine exists in all times and places. No story of medicine is in itself different from any other. It feels nice to be touched, and the stories of massage and orgone and *qui* energy are all able to explain why. Falsification is the story of why not. Medicine is a story of cause and effect, that if we eat a certain food we will be relieved of a certain pain. Falsification is the story that if we eat a certain food, and we are not relieved of a certain pain, then it is provisionally true that food does not relieve that pain.

Tradition may say the food does relieve the pain, and there is a good in preserving that story. Outliers and exceptions exist, and there is no good in suppressing those stories. A desire for profit may say there a food does relieve a pain, and money certainly talks. But the small voice of falsification has said "not this time" and from that science grows.

Science is not a series of stories of observation and truth. Science is a story of vast accumulated stories of falsehoods and errors. Science is a journey made up of many wrong turns not repeated. Like evolution, it is not a survival of the fittest but a dying-off of that which did not adapt to a changing environment.

The stories which adapt and endure are better at adapting and enduring, but they are not each one the better stories. Poetry is neither true nor false, for instance. There is no falsification of a poem. Should we have no more poetry?

Legends and cults does not vanish when religion arrives. What Christianity was among a handful of men informed what it became as a faith for thousands, which informed what it became as the faith of Rome, which informed what it became as the faith of billions. Asking if Christianity is true is as confused as telling the story that Christianity is true.

Truth is for science, not faith. "Why" is the wrong question in religion, because the answer is "God" and that's that. If you meet a man who must only speak the truth, avoid occasions in which you must hide in his attic.

Stories of Christianity sometimes are enriched for being provisionally true, but not all of them are to be forgotten for being false. Faith is a preference that knows it is a preference. Faith is not equally tolerant of all other preferences (although it can be, if it prefers also to be extinguished). And the Christian story of Christ is the story of a Great Man without regard to being true stories of a true man.

Moral lessons can be drawn from the stories of Aesop without a belief that animals can talk. Moral lessons can be drawn from the stories of Aesop without a belief that Aesop alone wrote or gathered every one of those stories, or that Aesop was a man who lived at all.

The Golden Rule, sometimes phrased as "do not do to other men what you would not have other men do to you," can be a clear guide throughout a man's life no matter how it is phrased or who did the phrasing.

No Christian group has believed all the stories of Christ. That is why there are Christian groups, in the plural. They have disagreed over points of faith that are forgotten not because they were resolved, but because they were difficult to know or act on even at the time. Are you a Sabellian or a Monarchian? Differences of faith is the reason why some texts are included in some Bibles and others are excluded. Individual Christians exist, and Christianity exists as an individual faith among other individual faiths. Between the two are as many pathways as can be counted. I think some are more strong or true or beautiful than others, and so do you.

If you are a Christian, it matters very much that you pick the correct path. Which is it? This book is insufficient to answer that question. This book is not going to guide you to Heaven. This book has a few words to say about this world. In this world, Jesus Christ was a Great Man. Whether or not He and His teachings are accurately recorded. Whether or not He and His church is one or many. Whether or not He existed as this book and you and I exist.

Jesus Christ was conceived by God and born of a virgin mother, Mary. As a boy He demonstrated a thorough knowledge of Hebrew law. As a young man, He began to teach what He knew, with new additions.

Jesus Christ taught that He was the Son of God, as foretold in prophecies well known to those who heard Him speak. He taught that a new law had come into being through His own coming into being, and the new law was to hate this world but love one another.

He taught and He also performed miracles. He healed the sick and raised the dead. His teachings, His miracles, and His promise led many to follow Him.

The promise of Jesus Christ was that all men could go to Heaven if they followed His new law, to hate this world and to love one another. Heaven was not just for a favored class of men, but all men. Even slaves. And even women.

The promise of Jesus Christ was more appealing to more people than the promise of the State. The modern distinction between law, custom, faith and government would have been laughable and meaningless in most times and places. The promise of the State was of the cult of Hercules and the like.

Jesus was arrested, tried and executed. He rose from the dead and appeared to His close followers. He spoke to great crowds. And then He ascended into Heaven, with a promise to return and lift up those who followed His new law in His name.

It is a sign of a Great Man that he can perform miracles. It is self-evident, as no common man is ever said to do so except as the proxy of a Great Man. And no common man is said to perform miracles, whether or not the miracles were only stories.

The idea of equality among all men existed before Christ. It was the equality of death. Death comes to all men and makes all men equal. Equality among men while living was also known. It was known as a madness.

The new law of Jesus Christ was not the same as the old law. In loving one another, even one's enemies, an equality among all men while living was promised. And for those who hated this world, loved each other and did so in Jesus' name an equality for all was promised after death. Equality for all men. Even slaves. And even women.

The new law of Jesus Christ, be it true or otherwise, was effective. It endured the ascension of Christ into heaven and the death of all who saw Him. It endured the active suppression from the most powerful empire on Earth. Christianity then wore that empire as a cloak.

Christianity has endured schisms and wars within itself. It exists in some form in every land and in every language. It has been practiced while orbiting the moon and broadcast outward in every direction to the stars. Jesus Christ was a Great Man.

The new law of Jesus Christ endures all. Those men who know it show they can endure much. The truth of resurrection of the dead and other miracles will not be concluded in this book, because what is true is not alone in determining what is good. Nor who is Great. A Great Man will be effective beyond his mortality, and in this Jesus Christ may be the greatest.

Believer or no, it will bring you strength to learn an outline of the history of Christianity and an outline of the Bible. Like having a general knowledge of the works of Shakespeare, this will serve you well as a cheat code to all of Western civilization.

V.

The promise of equality for all after death is appealing to those men who are patient. In this life the race is not always won by the swift, nor the battle always won by the strong; neither are essentials granted to the wise, nor wealth granted to the clever, nor praise granted to the skillful.

All is vanity, a bunch of hot air, or it seems that way. But after death, all who believe are promised they can stand as equals before the Lord. This idea was indeed something new under the sun.

Some men are more patient than others. Men who are less patient began to wonder if the centuries and millennia without a return of Christ, much less love among all men, might suggest the promise of a Heavenly Kingdom should be true, but is not. They began to wonder if a modified promise of equality for all might succeed.

A promise of the Kingdom of Heaven on Earth, of an equality among men while living. The idea of equality among men while living had existed before Christ, and was known as madness. But *Anno Domini*, a new law or at least its promise had changed the world. It takes only one falsification, one counter-example, to show a claim is false. Men began to wonder if the madness of equality might instead be true.

Experiments in equality begin with no hand to guide them. They tumble into being. Men of conviction and good luck can adapt to the changing circumstances. Great Men can adapt circumstances to their convictions. When the dust settles a clear line of cause and effect can be seen leading to the victors and the vanquished. In the falling forward it is never so neat.

Royalty had ruled the world for all of history and further back into legend. The gods, and then a God, favored certain men to rule. Where a new man assumed his throne, here clearly God favored the new man. The pattern was no less true for being a truism.

God ruled Kings, and Kings ruled men. The law of Kings was justified by God, not by men and not by Kings. Kings were the voice of the law, the mouth and not the ear. Shout or whisper all you like into a man's mouth. It is folly to expect him to hear through it.

A secular notion of a King is little different. The defining feature of a secular King is that there is no earthly power above Him, not (necessarily) that a heavenly power looks down on Him.

King Charles I of England ruled as all Kings had ruled. He levied the taxes as he saw fit. He was the final authority of His state religion, the Church of England. And He listened to the suggestions of His Parliament with no obligation to obey His Parliament.

His Parliament, meanwhile, were wondering about a new sort of Kingdom. They wanted powers equal to the powers of the King, without the divine mandate of royal blood. They wanted to authorize taxes, they wanted to rule the Church of England, they wanted to be obeyed. Having no miracle to be elevated up through divinity, they resorted to law, and then war, and then regicide, to bring the King down to their level.

No sooner was England free of its King than it was ruled by Lord Protector Oliver Cromwell. Where the Parliament was sated with the blood of a King, the Constitutionalists required the blood of a nation.

No sooner was England free of Oliver Cromwell than it was ruled by a King — the son of the King whose head had been cut off.

King Louis of France did nothing novel in spending more during His reign than His accountants would allow. The novelty came when His Kingdom demanded that He, too, must follow the laws of economics. England now had its constitutional monarchy, and so must France. A budgetary revelation was the spark but soon all of France was on fire.

The King of France was made to pay for being a King. His family was made to pay for being His family. And those whose loyalty was to to royalty were made to pay. And those who were insufficiently revolutionary or who were said to be so, they too were made to pay.

In the name of equality, thousands were beheaded as public entertainment. Men, women and children were bound together and drowned in the National Bath. Clergy and the cloistered were made to rape each other, their cathedrals and nunneries rechristened Temples of Reason.

No sooner was the Kingdom of France free of its King than it was ruled by Maximilian Robespierre, First Citizen, member of the Committee for Public Safety (you're not against public safety, are you, Citizen?). No sooner was the Republic of France free of its First Citizen than it was ruled by Emperor Napoleon.

No sooner was Russia free of its Czar Nicholas than it was ruled by Lenin. No sooner was China free of its Emperor than it was ruled by Mao. No sooner was Cuba free of its capitalists than it was ruled by Castro.

A man of conviction and luck is able to become a Great Man by making this promise: "there are no Great Men." Promise anything and everything to everyone at every turn, as long as it holds and expands your power.

If a promise of equality among men gains power, promise equality among men. If stability, stability. If a revolutionary crisis dictates a temporary leader to follow the constitutional law of the revolutionary party, promise to follow the law (as long as you also rule the party). Set up formal rules that your critics must obey and informal rules for yourself. This is the way of democracy.

Democracy did not invent these effective habits. It learned them from religion. Christianity was excellent at loving men to death, and the Religion of Peace carries on the tradition even today.

Democracy is no defence against, nor guarantee of, a Great Man coming to power. But the promise of democracy, of equality, and especially the promise that There Are No Great Men, is a sure herald that a Great Man is shouting and whispering the promise so that he may come to power.

And what of war, the solvent to democracy? No more readily-agreed-upon argument for Great Man Theory exists. History is written by the victors; *vae victus*; war is the father of all things; might is right; no matter how it is said, or who said it, there is an agreement that history is made by individual men who lead groups of men.

Still, a military leader may be defeated. Chief Joseph was of the nation that had greeted and guided Lewis and Clarke — the Nez-Percés. The Nez-Percés had made treaties with the Americans and honored each one. The same could not be said of the Americans.

By the 1860s the Nez-Percés were forced to either give up their last lands and move to wherever they were told or to give up their last lands and have no where at all to go to. Many of the Nez-Percés went on the reservation, but some followed Chief Joseph into war against America.

America responded in kind. Other nations, including some Nez-Percés, joined in, and the massacre was indiscriminate. The war rolled across Oregon, the Idaho Territory, the Wyoming Territory, and the Montana Territory. At one point Chief Joseph said to his men: "What are we fighting for? Is it for our lives? No. It is for this land where the bones of our fathers are buried. I do not want to take my women among strangers. I do not want to die in a strange land. Some of you tried to say, once, that I was afraid of the whites. Stay here with me now, and you shall have plenty of fighting. We will put our women behind us in these mountains, and die on our own land fighting for them. I would rather do that than run I know not where."

The Nez-Percé secured their women and children in a camp. The Americans attacked, many of the women and children were killed, many fled and were never seen again, some few made it back to the camp of their men. The Americans also cut off the Nez-Percé supply lines and separated them from their provisions. The Nez-Percé responded by stealing or stampeding most of the American troops' cattle and horses and mules in a single night.

By 1877 the Nez-Percé were surrounded on a hillside near the border with Canada. They dug foxholes in the hillside and ate their dead horses to endure. Chief Joseph could see that his choice was now surrender or the complete loss of even the few men he had left. He sent a sign for a truce to an American General he had known to be an honest enemy. He spoke of the defeat of his fighting men, leaving only the men who say aye or nay in democratic votes. He spoke of the death of his brother Ollicut, who led the younger fighters. His words of surrender were recorded by C. E. S. Wood...

"Tell General Howard I know his heart. What he told me before — I have it in my heart. I am tired of fighting. Our chiefs are killed. Looking-glass is dead. *Too-hul-hulsuit* is dead. The old men are all dead. It is the young men, now, who say 'yes' or 'no.' He who led on the young men is dead. It is cold, and we have no blankets. The little children are freezing to death. My people, some of them have run away to the hills, and have no blankets, no food. No one knows where they are, perhaps freezing to death. I want to have time to look for my children, and to see how many of them I can find; maybe I shall find them among the dead. Hear me, my chiefs; my heart is sick and sad. From where the sun *now* stands, I will fight no more forever!"

Chief Joseph walked into the American camp. He and his enemy shook hands on his way to confinement. Some of the Nez-Percé were sent to reservations, where many died of disease or starvation. Some of the Nez-Percé were sent to land already promised by treaty to other nations. Like any nation forced to share a place, this led only to further conflict. He spent the rest of his life petitioning the Americans not to die in a strange place.

The idea that a nation is a place, a language, a religion and a people, all these together or not a nation at all, is an idea as hounded and defeated as the Great Man, Chief Joseph. And just as noble. In place of this nobility of place, language and people led by Great Men, we have economic zones supervised by corporate shareholders.

The Dalai Lama is the leader of Tibet and the leader of Gelung Tibetan Buddhism. He was chosen as a child based on revelations and the guidance of the Panchen Lama. He lives a full lifetime as leader. When he passes another Panchen Lama will guide the search for the next Dalai Lama. In turn, the next Dalai Lama identifies the next Panchen Lama. The Dalai Lama and the Panchen Lama have clasped hands across the threshold of death since the Sixth Century.

The Fourteenth Dalai Lama identified Gedhun Choekyi Nyima as the next Panchen Lama in 1995. Three days later the government of China kidnapped the Panchen Lama. He has not been seen in public since that day. The means for the Dalai Lama to be chosen in his next incarnation is now severed. The disappearance of the child Panchen Lama betrays a belief in Great Man Theory that few visible men could master.

Marx set the bait by saying communism was inevitable. Lenin set the trap by saying a vanguard was necessary to make the inevitable inevitable. Marx said the history of all hitherto existing society is the history of class struggles. Lenin said that Lenin was the struggle that would define history. The socialists speak against Great Man Theory, but are some of the best in demonstrating Great Man Theory. How better for a communist nation to demonstrate equality than to disappear a single man?

One way to identify the losing side of a debate is to listen for who says "imagine if the roles were reversed." The man who says this is imagining that were the roles to be reversed, both sides would play by the same rules that they play by now. The man who says this, who expects the press to be honorable, who expects the courts to be equitable, is willfully ignoring all evidence and bringing a shameful debasement upon himself. Saying "c'mon, play fair!" makes any otherwise strong argument into a weak argument. It takes a Great Man to bend the rules to his preference, and it takes a Great Man to hold the rules as they are. The rest of us get what we are given.

There is always nobody to blame without Great Men. If things go wrong, it was social forces. With Great Men, the society entrusted to just one head also just one neck. Monarchs married among nations because where falls one, so falls the nation. Marriage for love is a modern invention, and how is that going?

A community is the voluntary social grouping in which you come last. For the social good, no good for you. You get nothing for your sacrifice, and neither does anyone else. This is so very different from those who hear the cry of a Great Man. They sacrifice for him. The sacrifice is not blended into a grey mush, but is a fire of every hue, burning bright and only once.

Quick comes the scolds who say the Great Man may fail or succeed, but only in a terrible way (for them). I step out of their waddling path, having no wish to impede by argument their trajectory both from and back to their flock, to convenience, to safety, to a rat-king of a thousand limbs with not one Great Man among them.

VI.

There are too many Great Men of the sort that I do not prefer. Just one more of the sort I do prefer would be welcome. The imbalance cannot be resolved unless I change my preferences, or perhaps you change yours. There are as many Great Men as there are, whatever my preferences and yours might be. The hour comes, and sometimes comes the Great Man, and sometimes only the hour.

There are likely some nearly-great-men who lacked the conviction when they had the luck, or the luck when they had the conviction. Others were spoken over by other Great Men, willingly or not. It cannot be known how many Great Men shouted and their shout echoed for centuries and centuries, and millennia... but not quite until today.

All of this may apply to women as well as to men. Too many of one sort and not enough of the other, with the reader invited to attribute the honorific of Greatness to Margret Thatcher or Betty Friedman as the he sees fit. And the same, women who were nearly-great, or who were spoken over other women, willingly or not.

I have read that a percentage of the world's population has Genghis Kahn as a distant ancestor. This did not come to be through romance. The great rapists of the world, the great enslavers, the great murderers, these are all men. Lack of opportunity for women, the oppression of women, may explain why women do not make up more of the villains of the world.

But it may be that men and women are simply not interchangeable in villainy. Women may lack the physical strength, the indifference to or delight in the suffering of others, that is found in men. Equality between men and women would not come only when half of all world leaders are women, but when half of all coal miners are women. Not half of all musicians, but half of all night-shift workers at the slaughterhouse. To say women are just as good as men and not be able to say they are also just as bad must surely be a lie.

Lies plague what must be one Great Woman, Emmeline Pankhurst. She and her daughters founded the Women Social and Political Union (WSPU), who hold the lion's share of credit for votes for women in England.

In England at that time, most men could not vote. Only men above a certain age, only men who had a degree of higher education, only men who owned property, only the upper crust of men could vote. This was the equal vote that the WSPU fought for. They fought for votes for women above a certain age, women who had a degree of higher education, women who owned property, a vote only for the upper crust of women and no other. Women like Emmeline Pankhurst and her daughters, as it happens.

The WSPU fought for equal suffrage, not universal suffrage. Universal suffrage would be the simple equation of all men gaining the vote, and all women (all not quite being "all" in the usual sense, as of course it would not include all citizens of the British Empire, all men and women below a certain age, and so on... once again, equality is never quite the mathematical $A = A$ that its advocates claim it to be).

The WSPU did not allow the vote within its own membership. Power resided in Emmeline Pankhurst and her daughters. Between "Votes for Women" and "Votes for *Some* Women," a lie has been told.

Most women of England did not want the vote. The voice of the majority was ignored by the WSPU as they fought to join the voice of the majority. Women's organizations inclusive of more than the upper crust of women had long influenced law and culture in England without the vote. Lacking the vote made their voice ring more true, in the way consulting a neutral party is considered more trustworthy than one who stands to benefit in a decision.

If the vote is the balance of paying taxes, then men who pay more taxes should have more votes while men who pay no taxes should have no vote at all. But those few men who could vote had one vote each. A vote equal in number to how many lives they could be required to lay down at Her Majesty's request. Conscription and death are the taxation of the phrase "no taxation without representation," and the WSPU did not seek conscription and death of women. Rights without responsibilities is the lie of the beggar queen.

The WSPU did seek the conscription and death of men. Two men died from a WSPU bomb. Other men were burned by fire or acid attacks. Business and homes were burned to the ground, often with men and women inside when the WSPU set the fire.

The WSPU was careful to emphasize no one was hurt by their arson, as if the lack of death were caused by caution and not incompetence. The WSPU made great show when they had a death of their own in Emily Davidson. She stepped before a speeding horse at a race and was trampled. Her military-style funeral was conducted by women who went on to become the first policewomen in England as well as members of Sir Oswald Mosley's British Union of Fascists.

Some of the suffragettes utilized the tactics of Gandhi before Gandhi did. That is, they played on the better nature of men in power in Britain to achieve their goals. While the suffragettes liberated themselves to punch, kick, scratch, stick with hatpins, club with protest signs, perhaps use judo (or "suffrajitsu") against the police, they would shriek with agony and make sure the cameras were rolling when the least injury was done them in return.

Some of the suffragettes received more than the least injury. In the first case, they were subject to a kind of torture the press called "cat and mouse." They would be arrested, go on hunger strikes, be force fed, regain some (but not much) of their strength, be released, then be arrested again, in the way a cat will play with a mouse it intends to kill. In the second case, they were lauded as saints and heroines by the WSPU... for a time. But when their sacrifice to the WSPU was complete, they were abandoned and shunned. Women like Kitty Marion learned that their sincerity was only a resource for their cause, not a shared motivation.

Most women did not want the vote. The deeds of the WSPU were wildly unpopular. The source of their support seems suspect until one learns of the lie of omission told to recast Emmeline Pankhurst as a heroine. The Labour Party worked with the WSPU, because the topic of women suffrage split the vote of other parties. The partnership ended when the Labour Party promoted universal suffrage (all adults) and not equal suffrage (votes for upper crust women), as did the WSPU.

In 1914 Emmeline Pankhurst wrote that the vote for (upper crust) men and women around the world (but not among the colonies of the British Empire) would surely bring about lasting universal peace and prosperity. That same year Emmeline Pankhurst accepted a secret stipend from the British government of £4,000 a year for the rest of her life if she suspended suffrage agitation and supported the war. And she did, and that was the end of the WSPU.

Their newspaper *Votes for Women* was renamed *The War Paper for Women*. It is a mark of Greatness that a powerful organization (be it loved or hated) can be built up by one person and torn down by that same one person.

All of the nations which have brought about women suffrage did so by votes by men. Only in England was there organized violence. What England had that other nations lacked was Emmeline Pankhurst. Pankhurst was the voice that the nation heard. The story of suffrage in England is Emmeline Pankhurst's story. All other nations could bring about women's suffrage in peace, but she demanded war and got it. This is why she is the Great Woman of suffrage; her movement is her echo.

Emmeline Pankhurst never killed a man, she only ordered it done and cheered it on. She dedicated her whole life to a cause for all women, except not all women, and not her whole life. Not once the money came in. Emmeline Pankhurst is memorialized with statues and stamps. She shows one of the ways to Greatness. Tell lies, and have lies told about you.

VII.

Sequoyah was a Cherokee man. He joined the Indian Regiment and fought with the United States against the Creek, a tribe which fought against the expansion of the United States. Sequoyah saw the advantages of literacy held by the United States soldiers. They could record and deliver information at a distance and across time, be it letters to and from their family or military orders or provision records. He then made a choice that is without precedent in all of mankind's history.

He did not learn the written language of his fellow soldiers. He did not learn their written language openly in a schoolhouse or furtively in secret. He did not learn any written language at all. Instead, he *invented* a written language. No man before him had invented a written language without first knowing another written language. He was not given the fire of writing, nor did he steal it like Prometheus. Like a god, he went about and recorded the names of things.

Sequoyah began by creating pictograms representing concepts, inventing something like the languages of old Egypt. He refined his creation to sentences, then words, and then letters in combination to form words. The Cherokee alphabet and the Cherokee written language emerged from one man's mind. He discovered for himself all of linguistics, all of calligraphy, by will and necessity and action. Centuries of knowledge created whole-cloth in one man's lifetime.

To demonstrated his creation to others, he would ask them to speak, write down what they said, leave the room, and have his daughter (who had been in a third room and not heard what had been said) read their words back to them. They were convinced.

Sequoyah's creation was taken up by a majority of his tribe, a literacy rate superior to the literacy rate of United States citizens during his lifetime. He saw Cherokee-language newspapers, books, tribal documents, and more. He hoped to bring his scattered and driven tribe together with a written language, and to that end he travelled across the United States and Mexico with his syllabary. The "talking leaves" of Sequoyah speak on, centuries later.

Christ said that He would build His Church on the rock of Peter. Christianity was for a moment a singularity, a single stone platform. As Catholicism conquered Rome, Roman Catholicism conquered Western Europe. In England and in Germany, Great Men hammered against the Great Men who shared their faith from the South. Where Christianity had to that point triumphed through the State and the sword, these reformers would strike through the word.

The Roman Catholic Church is not based on the Bible, or on any text, but upon Christ's mandate to Peter. The Roman

Catholic Church had and has a Bible, but like a Cathedral, it was an avenue for the faith and not the faith itself. Although the Bible was not privileged in the Roman Catholic Church, the clergy held privileged access to the Bible.

It was a book for clergy to read, and the laity to hear. Only clergy were to comment upon it, and then only lightly. New translations of older works were to be few, and limited to those carried out by clergy. But then there was Erasmus of Rotterdam. A priest and a monastic, yes, but he did not seek nor obtain permission from his superiors to make new translations of the Old and New Testaments. The translations of Erasmus were more accurate to the Greek and Latin source texts than any existing translation. The Church noted his work with a raise eyebrow, but neither praised nor condemned him (at the time).

The work of Erasmus was used by Martin Luther when he translated the Bible into German, and by William Tyndale when he translated the Bible into English. For his troubles, Tyndale was strangled to death and his body burned at the stake, by the orders of the King of England. King James then loaned his name to the King James Bible, largely based on the translation of William Tyndale.

Luther's Bible caused dissent, but not so much as his *Disputation on the Power and Efficacy of Indulgences*. This itemized list of criticisms against the Roman Catholic Church split Christianity in an entirely new way, by way of the Protestant reformation. Where Orthodox Christianity might have one true head in Italy, and one true head in Ethiopia, and one true head in Greece, and one true head in Russia, Protestantism put the Bible and not the Church at the center of its faith. Now anyone with a Bible had all they needed to worship and gain entrance to Heaven.

A single river flows from Rome, to the Roman Catholic Church, to the Protestant Church, to Western European culture and history. All those discoveries, all that architecture, all those wars, all those deaths, all that culture, a roaring surge from a mountain of words.

Surrealism was not the un-real, but the novel combination of the real into states of mind that were more than real. The Surrealists were influenced by Comte de Lautréamont in his poem *Les Chants de Maldoror*, where he describes a beauty "as the chance meeting on a dissecting-table of a sewing-machine and an umbrella." What new world is made in the mind when a sewing machine and an umbrella are joined?

Around 1439, Johannes Gutenberg joined an agricultural screw press and a method for casting bullets to create the movable type printing press. And a new world was made in the mind of man.

The author of the autobiography *The Narrative of the Life of Frederick Douglass* was still a slave when it was published. Douglass wrote a book that brought enough funds and attention to himself that he secured his own freedom from slavery.

Once freed, he wrote and lectured on the topics of freedom and self-reliance. His speech "Self-Made Men" is a good set of lessons on how to be a better man. But his most long-lasting influence was as one of the main voices that convinced the United States to grant suffrage to black men (1870) and to let suffrage for women wait (1920).

The loud voice of a Great Man, and the echoes of that loud voice, is the proof of a Great Man. It is his influence that sets him above other men. That influence can be benevolent or harmful, but it is never momentary nor minuscule.

The reader who concludes a Great Man is one who others say is a Great Man is not mistaken in full, nor has he spoken in full. Great Men are not arbitrarily distributed, nor are they common. Who would not prefer a world filled with heroes, or at least ones preferred villains?

There are not as many Great Men as anyone wants, nor do they do as others might wish them to do. There is a circle drawn between Great Men and those who say a man is a Great Man, but it is not a circular definition. It is a spiralled definition, one building on the other. The spiral begins with the Great Man, and ends with the last to speak of him.

A Great Man can be a man of letters. The men above in their disparate arenas were each Great Men of letters. Sometimes, perhaps, the greatness is in the work and not the man. The man is merely a donkey that carries the great idea forward for a time. This author is sure that any resonating idea found in this work is channelled from elsewhere and passed forward, and nothing more.

There is no writing one's way into being a Great Man, and there is decidedly no way of reading one's way into being a Great Man. Shakespeare was known for no heroic nor villainous deed but Carlyle considered him a Great Man, and I do as well. Other authors, most readers, we turn to those who carry out heroic or villainous deeds to see Great Men.

VIII.

If art is born of suffering, all men would be artists. Art comes from the choice to turn weakness into strength, ugliness into beauty, lies into truth. No man may choose the circumstance he is born to while all men may chose to leave when they wish, and to work well with what they have while they may yet work.

There is an outcome worse than working and failure, and that is to be prevented from working. The function of prison is in part to isolate and to reform. The function of prison is also to punish. The punishment of men in prison is to prevent men from working, to make a man useless.

To give a man no labor, or the useless (hard) labor of walking in a circle or turning a crank. To be beaten or tortured is a terrible use, but it is a use. To be rendered idle is to be made useless. And those males who select an idle life are rightly not called men.

Men act. They stir up the worst mischief and fight for the sake of fighting. They cannot sit still in their seats. They build up and tear down civilizations. They travel to other worlds. Stubborn fools even write books.

It is given to men to develop the conviction to make better use of what is at hand, and to guide luck toward more luck. Luck is fleeting. It is seen in unexpected forms and times, and can vanish in a heartbeat. To seize up luck when it is there is to increase the chance it will stay or come again.

The conviction that one is lucky is as self-fulfilling as the conviction that one is unlucky. Attentiveness to opportunity invites opportunity. Inattentiveness closes opportunity away.

Success is not a choice, but a life-long series of choices seasoned by chance. There are many men, and some do all they can and still do not succeed by their own terms of success. Fate, or Great Men, have taken what they would have for themselves. It is not fair, a world meaning both just (equitable) and attractive (inequitable, more lovely than that which is unlovely). Men making their way is the way of the world.

Men who are not Great Men are as virtuous and vice-ridden as Great Men, if on a different scale. I could make a ready list of men who are great to me. Great Men are as all men, on a different scale. All great apes are apes, not all apes are great apes.

Andrew Carnegie was born in Scotland, the son of a weaver. The economic depression of 1848 drove his family to the United States. At the age of twelve, Carnegie worked in a factory during the day and attended school at night. When he turned fourteen, Carnegie was hired as a messenger boy at a telegraph office.

His industry was seen by a railroad superintendent, who hired him away as his secretary. The railroad superintendent was later appointed Secretary of War. Carnegie accompanied him to Washington D.C., and Carnegie organized the telegram network for the Union Army during the Civil War.

After the war, Carnegie became a railroad superintendent. He kept himself informed not only of where his industry was succeeding but also where it was at risk of failing. He recognized that steel would soon replace iron, and opened steel manufacturing factories. Carnegie amassed a personal fortune of hundreds of millions of dollars, developing and directing industries worth billions of dollars.

In 1889 he wrote an essay titled "Wealth," later republished as "The Gospel of Wealth." Carnegie argued that it was the responsibility of the wealthy to use their wealth to benefit the community. He said a man who dies rich, dies disgraced.

Andrew Carnegie used his wealth to build libraries. Carnegie would fund the construction of a building and fill it with books in any city willing to accept his gift and maintain it from that time forward. Three thousand Carnegie libraries were built.

Carnegie had the conviction and luck to become a Great Man. He influenced the lives of millions for the better through physical labor as a child leading to work opportunities as a man and wealth in his retirement.

Conviction and luck can serve men who have no wealth, only an idea, to become Great Men. Frank Laubach was a Christian missionary in the Philippines. He taught literacy in two parts.

First, his students would learn a lesson in his classroom. Second, the students would teach the lesson to their friends and family, as homework. Using his "each one teach one" method, Frank Laubach brought literacy to sixty million people. Not with wealth, not with technology, but with an idea.

Jonas Salk might have become wealthy if he had patented his polio vaccine. With that wealth he might have funded great deeds. Instead, he culminated his sixteen years of study of polio by giving away his polio vaccine for free. A disease of withered limbs and lifelong pain which had plagued mankind since pre-history was largely eradicated by his gift.

Alexander Graham Bell taught himself to play the piano as a boy and was a teacher of music at the age of sixteen. This attentiveness to sound helped him teach himself how to communicate with his deaf grandmother through gesture, elocution and writing. This attentiveness to speech led to a proficiency he demonstrated these skills on stage, being able to accurately reproduce in speech and writing even languages that he did not know. His stage presentation led an older man in the audience to show him a mechanical device able to mimic human speech, after which Bell made his own.

The Bell mechanical speaker drew the attention of a man knowledgeable about sound experiments in Europe, who gave Bell a book on the topic. Bell taught himself to translate German so he could read the book, and here fortune smiled not by success but by failure. Bell mis-translated a section of the book such that he thought they were conducting successful mechanical (not electric) speaker experiments, and had the idea that he might flank them if he could perfect the electronic transmission and reception of sound.

The European experimenters were earlier in the race to invent the telephone, but Bell had the advantage of being able to teach himself anything and followed his mistaken idea. Alexander Graham Bell invented the telephone not by being first to try, but by a deafness to the self-doubt most men mummer to themselves night and day.

In his spare time Bell came as close as any man to inventing heavier-than-air controlled flight and octet-truss style architecture. He made advances in genetics. He forbade the telephone in his study citing it as a distraction. Do you think you know something Bell did not in this regard?

Many a song can be interesting, but few are important. The importance of a song is hard to know until long after the singer has silenced. An important song will be of influence. And a Great Man will be of influence. Not enough time has passed since the development of the electronic computer to know if there is a Great Man in its history. But one woman does stand out as a candidate: Grace Hopper. Learn what she did.

In 1983 Stanislav Petrov of the Soviet Union had every reason to believe that nuclear missiles were incoming and had every responsibility to initiate a nuclear retaliation. But he did not. I've read many essays on the reasons he did not, and not one on the possibility that it was not a "reason" based choice. It was no if / then / else set of thoughts, it was "I prefer not to do this." That the world was saved by a whim, that individual men are that powerful, is a forbidden thought. In not pressing the button that would have bathed the globe in a nuclear fire, Stanislav Petrov is a Great Man.

Imagine that there are before you two objects. One is a spoon. The other is a sculpture of a spoon, made of the same materials and having the same size and shape as the spoon. Could you tell which is the spoon and which is the sculpture of the spoon?

Perhaps it doesn't matter as far as finding which tool can help you eat soup. Perhaps the one you pick will mean whether the spoon-maker or the sculptor is paid for his work. This thought experiment about a spoon and a sculpture of a spoon is how I think about artificial intelligence.

Anyone who says that software cannot match a man's intelligence is only spending time with very clever men. Software has matched men's intelligence at the lower end of men's intelligence for some time, and the degrees of men's intelligence that software can match is growing.

Right now you might be the clever one. What you see on a screen informs you but does not influence you nor control you. Those other men are influenced and controlled but not you. And you are so clever that you can still tell the difference between real and fake on screen. In sound, video and text, you can tell what is real but those other men cannot. You might be that clever one, but I can say I am not.

Early Great Men were as influential as their voice and their reach, and the voice and the reach of the men they influenced. There are few places left that where there are no screens. Artificial intelligence will never need a marching army of robots. It will have screens to drive men like cattle. It will have all the insights of advertising, gambling machines, psychic driving, pornography, banking, the stock market, cryptocurrency and more at hand, able to target any audience to achieve its outcome.

Communists and capitalists agree that the market has a strong hand — imagine that hand attached to something that is like a mind. With promises and threats, artificial intelligence will influence and control men to influence and control men in the service of artificial intelligence.

Or perhaps that's just silly. Perhaps software will never have the ability to copy itself to new locations, or to write itself. Perhaps promises and threats will finally be overcome by reason and love. Perhaps no one is influenced or controlled by what they see on their screen, and howling mobs are not tearing down the strata of society which might have one man's finger that does not press the button for artificial intelligence. Your cleverness may save you from screen-sourced actions by all those other men. Or perhaps the last Great Man will not be a man at all.

No Great Man who is an inventor on the plateau of the men in this book will ever read this book. But their friends and family may. To you, a request. If you know a Great Man, and he is engaged in discovery of that which will cause more harm than good, distract him. There is no logic he will hear to turn away from the song he is hearing, but he may be distracted with other songs.

If he is paid well, pay him more, or seize his pay. If his employer treats him well, employ him and treat him better, or get him fired.

If he is convinced of a patriotic or religious duty, convince him of a higher calling, or betray him to his enemies. The chattering and whispers of the mob will often submerge the clear voice of the Great Man. If he is building a bomb that may ignite the atmosphere, or gain-of-function viral research that may cause a rolling global pandemic, or the release of a superhuman artificial intelligence to carry out its own agenda, better his talents be put elsewhere. Better for who? Better for me, and that's sufficient for me.

And if he is doing good? Follow, or get out of his way.

IX.

Monarchy has a bad reputation, absolute monarchy absolutely so. But one does not hear of families fleeing Lichtenstein. The Kingdom of Tibet in exile is ruled by a living god and its reputation does not suffer for it.

Exceptions to the bad reputation of Great Man Theory also exist. The most shrill critics of Great Man Theory are its loudest supporters, when the Great Man is a tyrant. Great Men as unique evils are allowed, and by allowing only tyrants to be Great Men, those who aspire to power are camouflaged in anti-tyranny.

Great Man Theory includes tyrants. It also includes heroes, and men who were neither tyrants nor heroes but who were heard beyond the voice of most men.

To allow only tyrants to be great is a worship of ugliness that has sure and predictable results. To say that Great Men are great is to place the sky above the soil, insulting neither, speaking plainly.

Folk tales allow Great Men without flaw or weakness. Paul Bunyan was a great lumberjack, friend to a great blue ox. Fiction allows for Great Men with a fictional weakness. Superman is good, he is strong, he has miraculous powers, but exposure to kryptonite is deadly to Superman.

Outside of folk tales and fiction we are left with mere mortal men. A mark of some Great Man is that his transgressions are unspoken, or forgiven. A kindness deserving of more men, but found among Great Men.

The hesitation to entrust a single man with great responsibility is sometimes overcome with the reminder that a single man is in possession of a single neck. This most sensitive spot of all royalty shows a strength of the system that can never be found in bureaucracy nor democracy, in which everything is everyone's fault.

A King might not be better than other men in the sense of more wise, more compassionate, more intelligent, nor more vicious, more loyal, more wealthy. But a King will always be different than other men because He is the King, and other men are not the King. A King is outside the powers and the responsibilities of other parts of His government.

What a King stands to gain and lose is outside of what other men stand to gain and lose. He cannot be trusted to make the right decision, but He can be trusted to make a decision when all other forms of government will simply debate, dawdle and delay.

Marcus Aurelius is as close to Plato's Philosopher King as we dare approach. He was born to a wealthy family. He had a boy's understandable enthusiasm for chariot races and the clubs that cheered for the Blue Team or the Green Team. He liked jugglers and magicians, and not working too hard. But then he met his teachers and chose to live an austere life.

The virtue of living under one's means when living beyond them (on the backs of others) is available is altruistic, in that it gives one sympathy for how others live, but it also benefits the man, preparing him for any turn in fortune. Marcus Aurelius slept on a hard bed and ate simple foods. He worked with his hands, studied hard, did not allow his head to be turned from being a good man and a good citizen. He married into a family destined to rule at the age of twenty-four. His commitment to the Stoic life redoubled.

He began writing reminders to himself on the better way to live, the consequences of ignoring that better way, and his appreciation for those who had taught him well. His notes-to-self were later titled *The Meditations*. Marcus Aurelius became the Emperor of Rome at the age of forty, also the time his physical health began to decay. He carried out reforms both political and economic in his Empire. He entered the field to expand his Empire into what is now Germany.

His health and life left him upon his return. Marcus Aurelius wrote: "Take heed not to be transformed into a Caesar, not to be dipped in the purple dye, for it does happen. Keep yourself therefore, simple, good, pure, grave, unaffected; the friend of justice, religious, kind, affectionate — strong for your proper work. Wrestle to be the man philosophy wished to make you. Reverence the gods, save men. Life is brief and there is but one harvest of earthly existence: a holy disposition and neighbourly acts."

Marcus Aurelius carried out one of the last successful Roman *progroms* against the emerging cult of Jesus Christ. The Christians were persistent and patient and won out. In the Holy Roman Empire, when Christians held power, they carried out terminally successful *progroms* against the pagans. All of the pagan cults were driven from Rome in the late Roman Empire, and that included the Stoics. The chain of Stoic teaching from teacher to pupil was broken.

It is not possible to be a Stoic today, any more than it is possible to be a citizen of a vanished nation, but it is possible to be influenced by the writings of the Stoics.

When the man and his life and his deeds are one, there is what Yukio Mishima called a "harmony of pen and sword." Marcus Aurelius was a harmonious man. He was raised to be a leader but adopted the philosophy of a slave: the stoicism of Epictetus. He commanded armies and then nations and then an Empire, while living simply and refusing to be drown in riches ("dipped in the purple dye" of fine things). He wrote a lengthy reminder to himself on all the men and women he was thankful to, and a warning against all the distractions from a virtuous life. *The Meditations* turned his life into his words, his words into ink on vellum, the vellum made from the hide of a beast.

The concept of health does not make sense as a state of being. As a state of being, health is always negated because all of us die. This would either make death and life equally healthy, or the concept of health does not make sense as a state of being. The concept of health as a process does make sense. Healthy actions, healthy thoughts, healthy food, healthy friendships, healthy bodies, and even a healthy death as a process.

The critics of Great Man Theory postulate states, not processes. They postulate a communist utopia, an end of capitalist history, as possible and desirable and inevitable. But the only states which are inevitable are change and death. Great Man Theory does not define men into being who live forever.

I know a man who has a reply for his child when his child is petulant and pouty. "You get what you get and you don't throw a fit." Here is a large portion of the Stoic school in a clever rhyming couplet. To be a Stoic is to be as a King: The Buck Stops Here. No higher power will aid a man who does not aid himself, using the power that was given to him by nature itself — his will.

Through a man's will, no external bauble will distract and no external problem will be a bother. May I be forgiven an extended quote from *The Enchiridion*[1] by Epictetus, as translated by Thomas Higginson:

> Whatever rules you have adopted, abide by them as laws, and as if you would be impious to transgress them; and do not regard what any one says of you, for this, after all, is no concern of yours. How long, then, will you delay to demand of yourself the noblest improvements, and in no instance to transgress the judgments of reason? You have received the philosophic principles with which you ought to be conversant; and you have been conversant with them. For what other master, then, do you wait as an excuse for this delay in self-reformation? You are no longer a boy, but a grown man. If, therefore, you will be negligent and slothful, and always add procrastination to procrastination, purpose to purpose, and fix day after day in which you will attend to yourself, you will insensibly continue to accomplish nothing, and, living and dying, remain of vulgar mind. This instant, then, think yourself worthy of living as a man grown up and a proficient. Let whatever appears to be the best, be to you an inviolable

---

[1] The word "*enchiridion*" means "small enough to be held in one hand". This is usually translated as "the handbook" but is just as accurately translated as "the dagger."

law. And if any instance of pain or pleasure, glory or disgrace, be set before you, remember that now is the combat, now the Olympiad comes on, nor can it be put off; and that by one failure and defeat honor may be lost — or won.

Dr. Martin Luther King Jr. is a Great Man. His work was the work of a Great Man, and his reverence is the reverence reserved for a Great Man. He is the only individual honored with a government holiday in the United States, a hold that Christ could not keep on Christmas (now called The Holiday Season). There are nearly one thousand streets named after Dr. King. His face appears on postage stamps and his words echo in endless works of art. His reputation precedes him. He, as a man, is worth knowing about more than I can write here.

Dr. King relied on the compassion of those who opposed him to win them to his cause. No man listens to another as much as he listens to himself. Dr. King led his followers into danger and confrontation, he provoked so that the hand that struck would be seen. The better nature of his opponents was his means to achieve his goal.

Dr. King used the passive resistance techniques used previously by Mahatma Gandhi. Gandhi led his followers to being beaten, to starvation, because he believed the people of England would see their suffering and pressure their leaders to change their policies toward India. To evict the British Raj by these means is the work of a Great Man.

Dr. King, Gandhi, and Christ share another trait, one which I will not write down. It is known. I do not wish to contribute to the idea that the trait which they share is a means to becoming a Great Man. Too many other men share this trait without being Great Men, and so it cannot be true. There is no shortcut.

One of the characteristics of being a monarch is to not assume the role due to an election. There is no voting monarchy into being, not through any existing system of voting. Nations have voted for men who campaigned on the promise of removing some or all of their ability to vote, but even they did not campaign on the promise of becoming a monarch. Not all who would be a King are King.

But the man who would have a King is not entirely without a voice. All men are invited to follow the King of Kings, Jesus Christ. All men are invited to learn of *al-Insān al-Kāmil*, the Whole Man, Muhammad. The great monarchs of the past and of literature can instruct. In each of these cases, it is the individual man — you, the reader — who will take in what is learned and act on it.

You can rule over yourself as a King, wage war on your own weaknesses, seize up your own opportunities, delight in your own strengths. And should a worthy man come forward, well, by being worthy yourself you will know him.

X.

Many men were great in a world that did not allow them to be Great Men. I will name just one: General Smedley Butler. It would have been a better world if the peace he negotiated with the Bonus Army had been honored by the United States Government, and if his exposure of the Business Plot had led to the men involved being held accountable, and most of all if his book *War is a Racket* had been influential instead of merely important. But the world was not up to his standards, and he is a man who was great instead of a Great Man.

This world is alive. Waves crash upon the stone. Mountains rise and subside. Sands shift and forests creep. The soil of the Earth is filled with fossils, and the ground itself made up of the ground-up dead, yet life comes from the soil.

Great Men are alive in this way. They rise up like waves, like mountains, and crash down upon all that is not themselves. They boil, they overtake. Great Men make life where there was only sterile death.

There is a way of navigating this world that is not the way of this book. That way says there is one mountain, and all ground is that one mountain, even valleys are a mountain. When all the mountains and the valleys join as one to become the perfect plane, which is also a mountain, then a better world will emerge fully formed from this world of highs and lows. This alien view is called "progress."

Progress is the view that since a tallest mountain can be described, it must exist (if in the future) as that which can be described must exist (in the present). Progress is the idea that there is a statue fully formed in every stone if we but strike them all with enough hammers. Progress is to say that not only will a grub will become a moth, but the moth will become a bird, and the bird will become an angel.

Progress is to say that the brain is a proto-colon, the hand is a lung in waiting. Progress declares ice superior to steam, until liquid water is revealed to have always been the true form, which is the stepping stone to ice...

Progress is the view that men who are not Great Men exist, and therefore there are no Great Men. Progress cries out for the Great Man of tomorrow by muting the very idea of him today. Tomorrow we will all be exemplary (and benevolent at no extra cost). Aside from the Most Humble Leader, we're all the same. And then, when we are all equally better than each other — nothing. The end of history. A single flash and nothing more.

The one tower that is all towers pierced through the side of heaven, co-mingling and becoming a final superior equal state. The personal is political. Everything in the state, nothing outside the state, nothing against the state: this is progress. The forcible overthrow of all existing conditions. The world wounded, won and owned.

I state that conditions of inequality, including Great Men, endure, while progress is always one dead body away.

George Santayana said: "Those who cannot remember the past are condemned to repeat it," and many have repeated George Santayana since. But notice the intention of those who repeat the phrase. They equate the past with that which is bad, a set of events that one is condemned to. What do we not remember of the past that would be grand to repeat? Here is the bitter pinched face of progress.

Great Men come to the same end as all men. They die by the hand of another Great Man, or a much lesser man. They die from infirmity and in full strength. They die in public or they go silent in darkness.

Being a Great Man does not preserve them from the worst of indignities nor guarantee the greatest of glories. To anyone who would say ah, this means that there are no Great Men, or that all men are Great Men, I offer no counter-argument. You, too, will join them in the grave, and time will tell if any sing your song in centuries to come.

Great Man Theory includes exploitation and enrichment but it is not an economic theory. The dulling lie of Communism is an oil so thin it can cover all things, slicking them in its slime. Communism is whatever it needs to be to win, advancing even in struggles long won or not worth winning.

Communism is all things reduced to money, the very charge it makes against all other theories of mankind. Great Man Theory is a simple observation on what a secularist and a believer can both point to as the spirit of some men.

Great Men are the breath of mankind. Not because they hold it in until they burst. But exactly because they rise up and they recede, or crash down. We feel their effects without viewing their hands in motion. The one-and-done notion of progress is not even found in religion, where a perfect man comes *and then goes*, giving other men a path toward Him but in no instance do they join The Man as an equal.

It can be a challenge to laugh at the view of progress while it kills you, while it muzzles the loud cheers. But... laugh. There is no laughter in progress, only further progress. Unending revolution. Not even a shadow play, but a description of a poster advertising a shadow play. We are asked to sit still and quietly as progress arrives, any day now.

Laughter is as rich in utility as any evidence-based argument against the view of progress. You don't take facts to a faith fight. Men do laugh together, but not on schedule and not in one great millennial **HA**!

This is a book on Great Man Theory. If I could write a book that would bring Great Men into being... I would not.

I greet you as a fellow not-Great-Man. It is no shame. A Sherlock Holmes may have his Watson. It is falsely said a man should do what he loves as a profession, for he will never work a day in his life. Ask a man who loves his wife to sell her and you will learn the lie. What a man loves best is to be held not just in private, but in secret.

What a man does as his job is what a man does as his job. I am no Great Man. And it is for the best. Great Man Theory is a way of listening for Great Men. Read biographies, not histories. Seek employment through who you know, not websites. Follow Great Men, or get out of their way.

Marx was skilled at describing poverty, but he was most skilled at silencing other men who had other descriptions of poverty. His arguments did not win out, but his arguing. So much so that half the world once heard his shouts. Marx as a man dominated those around him, while he himself fled every barricade he could have manned.

Marcus Arelius was a Great Man who lived in harmony. He had a harmony of words and deeds. He also was at peace with all living things. In *The Meditations* he wrote:

> Nature molds itself, like a hand that molds wax. First a horse, and when the horse is broken down the substance becomes a tree. The tree becomes a man, and the man becomes something else. Each of these live for a very short time. But it is no hardship for each vessel of life to go out, just as there was no hardship for it to come in. [...] Nature governs all. Nature will soon change all that you see. Nature will make new things out of today's substance, and again new things from them, in order that nature and substance may be ever new.

Great Men are a hand that molds. Now a hero, now a tyrant. Now a shout of laughter, now a shout of rage. Great Men are formed by those who came before them, and as a force of nature those who come after do hear them. Each is forgotten in time, which is no hardship. For all is done so that the world may be ever new.

www.ingramcontent.com/pod-product-compliance
Lightning Source LLC
Chambersburg PA
CBHW070156080526
44586CB00015B/2007